Discover other cultures

Toys and Dolls
Around The World

Meryl Doney

FRANKLIN WATTS
LONDON•SYDNEY

About this book

So many different toys are enjoyed by children around the world that it would take several books to cover all of them. Here we have chosen a few toys from a variety of countries, to give you an idea of the wide range.

The book begins with simple toys made out of natural objects, like the painted stones from Haiti. It goes on to look at some of the ingenious moving toys made by children in Mexico, India and South America. No one can write about toys without mentioning dolls, and we have a section which draws on the thousands available. Bicycles, cars, trucks and aeroplanes represent the many forms of toy transport that are made and enjoyed by their owners. Finally, there is the wonderful world of kites, in which people can play together as well as compete against one another.

Most of the steps used to make the toys are very easy to follow, but where you see this sign ask for help from an adult.

Children often use the simple materials around them to make their toys. They are very skilful at recycling things. The wire plane from Zimbabwe and the bottle-top snake from Mexico are good examples. See what you can invent with the objects around you, such as natural materials, household goods or discarded packaging.

A toy collection

If you enjoy making the toys in this book, you might like to start a toy collection. Explore craft and charity shops, cultural centres and specialist toy shops to see what you can find. And, of course, if relatives or friends go abroad, they may be able to bring back an unusual toy for you. You could begin with toys from one country, or start a collection of one sort of toy, for example dolls or *tap taps* (see page 24). Learn more about your toy collection by finding books on the history of toys from different countries at your local library.

Originally published as World Crafts: Toys and Dolls

This edition first published in 2002
© Franklin Watts 1995, 2002
Text © Meryl Doney 1995

Franklin Watts
96 Leonard Street, London EC2A 4XD

Franklin Watts Australia
56 O'Riordan Street, Alexandria, NSW 2015

ISBN: 0 7496 4546 6 (pbk)
Dewey Decimal Classification Number 745.592

Series editor: Annabel Martin
Editor: Jane Walker
Design: Visual Image
Cover design: Mike Davis
Artwork: Ruth Levy
Photography: Peter Millard

With special thanks to Alison Croft, educational advisor and toy maker.

A CIP catalogue record for this book is available from the British Library.

Printed in Dubai.

Contents

The world of toys

Toys must have been around for as long as there have been children to play with them. Bone whistles and fragments of small clay figures which may have been used as toys have been found. Some date back to the Stone Age.

More definite evidence has been found in China, dating from around 5000 BC, and in India and ancient Egypt. In Thebes, on Egypt's River Nile, pull-along crocodiles, leopards and jointed dolls were buried in tombs. By the time of the Greek and Roman civilisations, toys were well known.

Since these early times, toys have continued to be developed all over the world, because children love to play. Some toys have a double function, like the African dolls that are given as toys but are also meant to act as powerful charms to ward off evil. Toys also help to prepare children for the world of adults. In Indonesia, as soon as a baby smiles he or she is given gifts: a miniature wooden shield, sword and spear for a boy, a fireplace and cooking equipment for a girl.

During the eighteenth century, European reformers like Friedrich Fröbel began to realise the educational value of toys such as bricks, puzzles and games. From then on, toys became an important part of school life.

Today, most children's toys are manufactured and sold all over the world. But there is also great interest in traditional toys. We hope you will enjoy inventing your own toys, using some of these techniques, and sharing them with your friends.

Your own toy-making kit

As you begin making your toys, look around for odd bits of material, buttons, cardboard tubes and yoghurt pots. Keep these items in a box with a set of tools ready for when you want to make a toy.

Make some dough from the recipe below and store that too. Wrap it in cling film and keep it in a container with a tight lid.

Here are some of the most useful items for your toy-making kit:

hammer · tenon saw · hacksaw · awl · hand drill · needle-nosed pliers · scissors · craft knife · metal ruler · brushes · white emulsion · poster paints · varnish · PVA (white) glue · tube of strong glue · plastic modelling material · modelling clay · sticky tape · masking tape · card · paper · tissue paper · newspaper · pen · pencil · felt pens · fabric and felt · needle and thread · decorations, including sequins, braid, tin foil, sticky shapes and beads · newspaper to work on · card to cut on · apron · paper towels for cleaning up

Potato dough

This dough recipe comes from Peru. It is made from mashed potatoes and plaster of Paris.

3 tablespoons of instant mashed potato
10 tablespoons of plaster of Paris
water

In a small bowl, mix up the mashed potato with 150 ml of boiling water. Beat with a fork until floury.

In a larger bowl, mix the plaster with 3 tablespoons of cold water. Stir with a spoon until smooth.

Add the potato to the plaster and mix well. Form into a dough and knead well.

No cooking is required for this dough.

Papier mâché

'Papier mâché' means chewed paper! But don't worry, this method only involves building up many layers of glued paper over an existing object or model.

Cover the object you wish to copy with petroleum jelly to stop the paper sticking to it.

Mix one tablespoon of PVA glue with a little water in a bowl. Tear a sheet of newspaper into small squares. Dip a paintbrush in the glue and pick up a square with it. Lay it in place on the model and paint some glue over it.

Add more and more squares in this way until the whole model is covered.

Repeat this process several times. Leave in a warm, airy place to dry.

Simple toys

Catching a
ball may well
have been the
very first game
played by children. There
are pictures of balls being
thrown on Egyptian tomb
paintings and carvings, on Greek
vases and on Roman murals. The balls
were made from wood, rubber or feathers
bound with leather. Some were sewn from
rags, wound from strands of wool or cotton or
even formed of compressed cow dung. The bamboo
ball above was made in
Thailand, and the crocheted
cotton one (right) is in the
colours of South Africa.

Figures and creatures that are
made from natural objects are
equally easy to make and play with.
These brightly painted stones come
from the Caribbean island of Haiti.
The pebbles have been collected
from the beach and are painted as
imaginary fish.

Maybe the shape of a stick gave a South
African child the idea for the curvy snake. It is
simply whittled with a craft knife and painted.

Make painted stone creatures

Find a stone or pebble that has an unusual shape. If you are visiting the beach, a pebble will be ideal. Look at it from all angles and see if its shape suggests a person's face, or perhaps an animal, bird or fish. If you paint the stone white first, it will be easier to see its shape clearly.

You will need: stone or pebble · white emulsion · pencil · paints · felt pen · varnish · paper · glue · materials for decoration: card, clay, dough, papier mâché, sequins, beads, coloured paper, string, cotton wool, raffia

1 Paint your stone with white emulsion.

2 Draw in pencil the shapes you want on your stone. Fill in the shapes by painting areas of colour. Keep your design simple and bold.

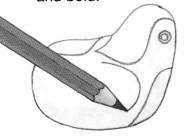

3 When the paint is dry, neaten the edges by going over the original pencil lines with a felt pen. Add a coat of varnish.

4 The brightly coloured bird has a paper beak. Roll a piece of paper into a cone shape. Use strong glue to attach it to the stone.

5 You could add any number of extra features to your creature, like wings, a tail, scales, fins, ears or a nose. Use materials such as beads, string, wool and raffia.

You could make a snake, lizard or crocodile from an interestingly shaped stick. Choose a piece of old dry wood. Strip off the bark and shape the stick roughly with a penknife. Add details, and paint as for the stone creatures.

Toys with bobbing heads

Toys with bobbing heads are produced in many different areas of the world. They are made by finding an object's perfect balancing point. The tortoise was made from a walnut shell in the Indian state of Bihar. Its legs are pieces of wood from an old packing case. The carved wooden head and tail are suspended by wire loops so they can nod and wave when you touch them.

The same principle was used to make the colourful little aardvark from India. His body is a small seed pod and his tail is its stalk. The head and legs are twigs but the aardvark's ears are snippets of red plastic.

Make Aard the Vark

1 With a pencil, mark four points for legs, 1 cm apart, on either side of the table tennis ball seam. Draw a circle, 1 cm in diameter, for the head hole as shown. Mark a point on the bottom of the ball for the tail.

2 To cut out the head hole, carefully pierce with a pin and then use small pointed scissors. Pierce holes in all the other marks. Insert matches to form four legs and a tail. Glue in place, making sure Aard stands up firmly.

3 With a craft knife, remove bark and sharpen the end of the twig. (Always work away from yourself.) Paint on nose and eyes. Paint body and legs. Cut two tiny ear shapes from card or plastic. Glue in position.

4 Tie thread around middle of twig and hold it up. Move knot along until the head balances perfectly. Glue in place.

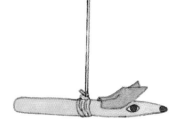

5 Thread needle and push it in through the head hole and out through the top of the ball. When the head balances in the centre of hole, glue thread in position on top of the body. Cut off extra thread.

Slithery snakes

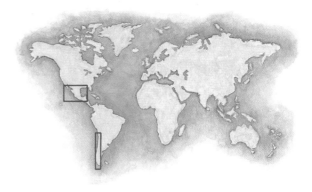

Snakes make great toys, probably because they fascinate children and are so easy to make.

Ruperto Monsalve runs a workshop in Villarrica, southern Chile, where he makes slithery crocodiles and snakes like the one shown below. The secret of their life-like movements is a strip of leather. It is glued along the length of the snake between the two halves.

The snake on the right is from Mexico. It has been made from metal bottle tops and corks. The face is painted to look menacing, and a long tongue is added.

Make a bottle-top snake

You will need: 100 metal bottle tops • plastic modelling material • awl • hammer • champagne cork • wine cork • craft knife • large needle • green garden string • felt pens

You will need about 100 bottle tops to make a good long snake. You could collect them from friends or at school. Or you might know someone who works behind a bar serving drinks in bottles. Give that person a large plastic tub with a lid and ask if the tops could be collected for you.

1 Place each bottle top, in turn, upside down on the plastic modelling material. Make a hole in each top by placing the awl in the centre and giving it a sharp tap with a hammer.

2 With a craft knife, shape the champagne cork into the snake's head.

Cut out a wedge-shaped mouth. Taper the wine cork so that it looks like the end of the snake's tail.

3 Thread the string through the eye of a large needle. Using the needle, thread the string through the mouth, each bottle top and finally the cork tail.

4 Knot the string at both ends. Leave it hanging out of the mouth to form the tongue. Decorate the face and tail with felt pens.

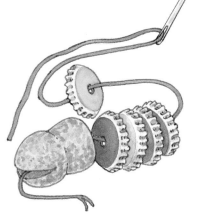

Wriggling toys

All over India, toy sellers can be seen offering a dazzling selection of brightly decorated toys. Many are made from the simplest of materials. As well as these toys which are made to sell, the ones that Indian children make for themselves are also very inventive. Children there use leaves, seeds, paper, cotton and anything else that comes to hand.

These fun toys from India are very simple to make from scraps, yet their mechanisms are quite sophisticated.

When the toy on the right is turned over, the four birds (or are they fish?) wriggle down the threads as though they were alive. Reverse the toy and off they go again.

The snake is driven by an elastic band and a small clay drum like a cotton reel. One pull on the string is enough to start the snake wiggling along the ground to frighten nervous relatives.

Make a wriggly snake

1 Model the clay into a roller in the shape of a cotton reel. Using a large needle, make two holes lengthways through the roller. Leave clay to harden.

You will need: a small piece of self-hardening clay (the size of a small cotton reel) • needle • scissors • card, 9 x 14 cm • flexible wire • pliers • thin elastic band • string • a long strip of computer paper • glue • ribbon • paints

2 Cut card into a head shape. Make two holes in both sides. Thread the wire through the holes, bending it to form a domed shape. Using pliers, twist the ends of the wire into hook shapes.

3 Cut open the elastic band. Wind string around the roller and thread through the head with the needle. Using the needle, thread the elastic band through one wire hook, one hole in the reel, the second hook and the second hole. Knot the elastic in place.

4 Cut out a strip of computer paper, 80 x 550 mm. Taper one end as shown. Fold paper in half lengthways, then into a concertina.

5 With the folded side towards you, gently push each concertina point inwards, by 5 mm, on alternate sides to form triangle shapes.

6 Open all the triangles and flatten the paper. Refold it along the zig-zag lines (marked in red) to form a 'bent' concertina.

7 Trim neck and glue to head. Add a ribbon tongue and tail. Paint and decorate.

Miniature world

There is great appeal in making tiny toys to treasure. The little scenes from every day life in El Salvador (below) are made from clay and painted.

The small woven basket has been made by hand in Ecuador. The brooch beside it is in the shape of a llama which is decorated with flowers.

The hair slide below is decorated with Guatemalan worry dolls. Guatemalan children keep these tiny dolls in a special box. Each one is a different character. The children tell one of their worries to each doll, and then hide the dolls under their pillow at night. In the morning the dolls have taken all their worries away!

Make a box of worry dolls

You will need: matches (used) • light card • strong glue • felt pens • short fabric strips • wool • fuse wire • empty matchbox • paint • fabric • button or tassel

The recipe on page 5 for uncooked potato dough is ideal for making your own miniatures or brooches. You could copy the ones shown opposite, or make scenes showing what life is like where you live.

1 Cut a matchstick in half. Wrap and glue light card around one end of the match to form a face. Draw on the face with felt pens. Wrap and glue fabric around the rest of the match to form the skirt.

2 To make arms, wrap wool tightly around a length of wire. Glue in place. Cut off a 3-cm piece for the arms. Glue to the doll's back.

3 Wrap wool diagonally several times across the upper body. Repeat the other way to secure the arms. Glue the end at the back.

Repeat this method to make as many more dolls as you want. Use different coloured fabrics and wools for the dolls.

4 Make a home for your dolls by decorating a matchbox with paint or fabric, and adding a button or tassel as a draw-pull. Line the box with a scrap of fabric.

These dolls have a matchbox home, but you can also use them as decorations. Glue them to an old hair slide. Or make a brooch by sticking the dolls onto a strip of cardboard and sewing a safety pin onto the back.

Dolls old and new

Dolls are found all over the world and in all cultures. They date back as far as civilisation itself. Dolls have been found in Africa, India, China, Mesopotamia (modern-day Iraq), ancient Egypt, Greece and Rome. The earliest dolls probably date back to Mesolithic times (around 10,000 years ago).

Fabric dolls like the one above have been discovered in tombs of the pre-Columbian Chancay people of central Peru. They date from around 100 BC to 1200 AD. They are a valuable part of Peru's history and so they are kept in museums and collections. Replica pre-Columbian dolls are still made for tourists to buy.

The Mozambican woman with a baby on her back and a bundle of firewood is made from fabric. By contrast, she is typical of the toys that are made for today's children to play with.

Make a mother and baby

It is very easy to make a copy of the ancient Peruvian doll shown opposite. The secret is strong tea! Before you begin, soak the fabric you plan to use in the tea over night. This will make it look old.

To make your doll, form a roll of flesh-coloured fabric and fold it in half. Wrap a stripy piece of fabric around the neck and sew in place. Add a little apron to hide the join. Draw or embroider the doll's face and sew on wool hair.

You will need: thick brown tights • scissors • dark thread • scraps of tights for stuffing • thick card circle, 9 cm in diameter • needle and thread • black wool • thick thread (for embroidery) • two pieces of African-style fabric, 40 x 17 cm • plain fabric, 22 x 22 cm • twigs

1 Cut the feet off the tights 30 cm from the toe. Put one piece inside the other. Stuff the toe to make the head. Wrap dark thread around the neck and tie.

2 Stuff the body and tie thread around the waist. Put card circle in the base and sew up the open end.

3 To make the arms, cut two pieces, 6 x 9 cm, from the tights. Fold each one in half, and then in half again. Sew across one end and down the side. Turn inside out and stuff. Fold in the ends and sew to the body.

4 To make the baby, cut an 8-cm square from the tights. Fold in half, and then in half again. Sew as for the arms. Sew up the open end. Tie thread around to form the neck.

5 To make the baby's hair, sew wool in and out of the head. Knot wool twice for each stitch. Use thick thread to embroider eyes and mouth on mother and baby.

6 Make clothes by hemming all around each piece of fabric. Wrap one patterned piece around the mother's body and tuck it in. The other forms a sling to hold the baby. Fold the plain fabric almost in half and tie around the head. Sew the bundle of twigs to the top of her head.

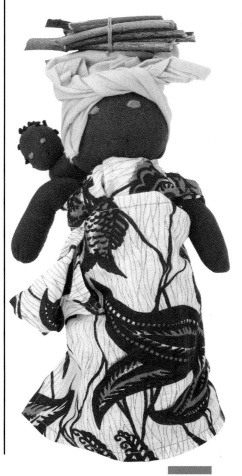

Peg dolls and apple grannies

Wooden dolls have been made all over Europe since earliest times. The most famous toy makers were those from Seiffen in Saxony, Germany, where wood carvers have been at work since the Middle Ages.

The simple wooden doll below was probably made in England, where the London-based toy-making industry began to develop after 1880. Later, dolls like her were made from hardwood clothes pegs and known as peg dolls.

The Pioneers who moved westwards across North America in the nineteenth century made dolls for their children. This unusual doll (left), called an apple granny, began as a young woman and then aged to become a grandmother within a few weeks. The secret of this magic is in the apple, which shrinks and makes the wrinkles on granny's face.

Make a doll from an apple

You can make a simple peg doll using a hardwood peg. Paint a face on the peg. Wind and glue a pipe cleaner around the body to form arms. Make clothes from scraps of felt and glue in place.

Choose a large apple to make your apple granny; you will be surprised how much it shrinks in a few weeks.

You will need: a large apple • vegetable knife • 3 tsp salt • bowl • cork • stiff card circle, 7 cm in diameter • PVA glue • chopstick • scissors • 9-cm strip of card • scraps of flesh-coloured felt • needle and thread • dress fabric, 14 x 34 cm • scraps of fabric, ribbon and lace • cotton wool • fabric circle, 11 cm in diameter • two beads • 11 cm of fuse wire

1 Peel apple. Use a vegetable knife to carve out the face. (Remember to cut away from your body.) Put apple in a small bowl, add salt and water to cover. Leave overnight.

2 Glue cork to centre of card circle. Make a hole in the cork and glue in the chopstick. When dry, push apple onto chopstick. Leave in warm, dry place for a few days.

3 Cut arms from the strip of card. Stick felt on each side and trim to shape. Glue arms to chopstick. Bind scraps of cloth around the body and sew in place.

4 Fold dress fabric in half and cut a T-shape. Cut hole for head. Sew up the sides (leaving armholes open) and hem. Put dress on doll, fold over and glue the neck edges. Make apron from a scrap of lace or cloth. Sew a 28-cm ribbon across top.

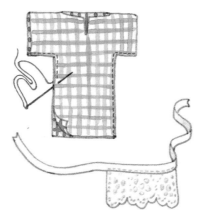

5 Stick on cotton wool for hair. To make hat, sew lace around edge of the fabric circle. Sew a circle of large stitches 2 cm from the edge. Pull this tight to gather up the fabric. Tie the ends of the thread.

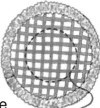

6 Stick a bead into each eyehole. To make glasses, loop wire twice around a pencil. Push ends of wire into sides of doll's head.

A nest of dolls

These nested dolls are traditionally called *Matryoshka* dolls. Today they are the best-known Russian dolls and are made all over Russia and the former Soviet Union. Surprisingly, however, the idea for small wooden figures that fit neatly into one another came originally from Japan. In the late nineteenth century the little figure of Daruma the Sage was brought from Japan to the Gorky region of Russia. A Russian artist, Sergei Malyutin, and a wood carver, Vladivere Zvezdochkin, transformed the figure into a set of Russian characters: six girls, one boy and a baby.

This set was made in Belarus. The dolls are dressed in traditional costume and decorated with a large, red flower. Red is a popular colour in Russia. It symbolises the rising and setting sun, the colour of strength and life.

Make five dolls in one

1 Form a doll shape 2.5 cm tall from plastic modelling material. Give it a flat base so that it stands firmly. Cover with several layers of papier mâché and leave to dry.

2 Roll out a thin layer of modelling material. Wrap it around first doll and form into a second doll shape. Add one layer of wet tissue paper. (This prevents your finished doll from sticking to the modelling material.) Add several layers of papier mâché and leave to dry.

3 Use a craft knife to cut through the outer layer of papier mâché at the widest point around the middle. Slip the two halves off the modelling material.

If this is difficult, dig out some of the modelling material with a penknife blade.

4 Remove thin layer of modelling material to reveal the first (smallest) doll.

5 Glue a strip of light card around the inside of the bottom half of the second doll, to form a lip. Replace the top half. Repeat this process with a second doll to make a third and so on. Make the dolls bigger each time.

6 Paint each doll with white emulsion. Decorate and varnish.

Wooden horses

Horses and donkeys were the main form of transport throughout Europe until the twentieth century. It is not surprising, therefore, that toy horses have always been popular with children. Model charioteers and horses on wheels have been found in burial sites from earliest times. Since then, horses have been made in all parts of the world, from the tiny painted wooden ones in India to the child-sized rocking horses of Europe.

The wood carvers of Europe are particularly known for their horses. The one on the right, with its red decoration, flowers and leaves, comes from the area around Lake Siljan in central Sweden. Wooden horses like these are so popular that they have become a symbol of Swedish design.

This pull-along cart comes from the Lachowice region of Poland. It is one of the simplest designs in a long tradition of wooden toys.

Make a horse-drawn cart

This toy is made with stiff cardboard and so it is not very strong. If you are good at woodwork, you could use the same pattern to make a much stronger cart from plywood.

You will need: a piece of graph paper · pencil and ruler · thick corrugated cardboard · sticky tape · craft knife · metal rule · strong glue · 1.5-cm dowel · awl · four 2-cm screws · white emulsion paint · poster paints · varnish

1 On graph paper, draw out patterns for cart as shown.

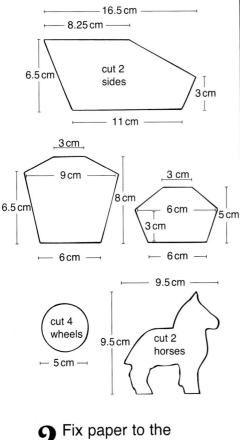

- 16.5 cm
- 8.25 cm
- 6.5 cm
- cut 2 sides
- 3 cm
- 11 cm

- 3 cm
- 9 cm
- 6.5 cm
- 8 cm
- 6 cm

- 3 cm
- 6 cm
- 3 cm
- 5 cm
- 6 cm

- cut 4 wheels
- 5 cm
- 9.5 cm
- 9.5 cm
- cut 2 horses

2 Fix paper to the cardboard with tape. Using a craft knife and metal rule, cut out all pieces plus a rectangle, 30 x 9 cm, for base. Cut off corners at one end of base.

3 Stick the front and back pieces between the two sides with strong glue. Glue cart and horses to base.

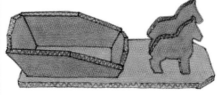

4 Cut two pieces of 1.5-cm dowel 11 cm long. Mark at 1 cm in from each end. Hold dowel firmly in vice. With craft knife, cut into dowel at both marks. Carve out wood in between the marks to form a flat surface. Repeat with second dowel.

5 Make a hole in the end of each dowel with an awl. Use a screwdriver to push a 2-cm screw through each wheel and into the end of the dowels.

6 Paint the whole cart with white emulsion and then decorate with poster paints. Varnish.

Brightly coloured transport

The tiny country of Haiti has no organised public transport, so a flamboyant system of privately owned trucks has developed. They are called *tap taps* (shown right), and are their owner's pride and joy. *Tap taps* are often painted in bright colours and decorated with Bible texts, prayers or slogans. Passengers are crammed inside and their luggage, produce and livestock are piled on top.

The same means of transport is popular in the villages of South America. There the open-sided wooden trucks are called *chivas*. Their decorations often depict wedding parties, religious processions or funerals. Pottery workers in the villages of Ecuador and Colombia make toy *chivas* for children (below right).

The tin truck (below centre) comes from Senegal in West Africa, and the wooden truck (below left) is from South Africa.

Make your own truck

Look closely at the trucks and vans on the facing page. They are made from papier mâché, clay, tin and wood. We have given instructions for making the wooden truck, but you may like to try your hand at making copies of the others, or inventing your own form of toy transport.

You will need: one piece of battening, 2 x 4.5 x 46 cm • one piece of wood, 1.5 x 7 x 35 cm • sandpaper • hammer • 16 2-cm nails • 2-cm quarter-dowel, 6 cm long • a length of 4-cm dowel • hand drill • white emulsion paint • poster paints • varnish • four washers • four 3.5-cm screws • wood glue

1 Mark the battening into four 7-cm and three 6-cm lengths.

Mark the wood into two 9-cm and one 17-cm lengths. Hold in vice and saw off lengths. Sand all edges smooth.

2 To form truck base, nail a 7-cm batten to each end of the 17-cm base.

3 To form truck body, nail two 7-cm pieces to a 9-cm piece. Turn over and nail the other 9-cm piece onto the ends, forming a box.

4 To form cab, stack two 6-cm battens on top of each other and nail together. Turn over, add the third 6-cm batten and nail. Nail the quarter-dowel to the top of the stack.

5 To make the wheels, hold the 4-cm dowel in the vice and saw off four 1.5-cm pieces from the end. Pencil a mark in the centre of each wheel, hold in the vice and drill a hole.

6 Paint all pieces with white emulsion and poster paint. Varnish. When dry, screw each wheel to base, with washers in between. Glue cab and back onto base.

Aeroplanes and bicycles

Here are some more examples of ingenious toys. These ones were made from wire in Zimbabwe. The aeroplane was made by two craftsmen, Enock and Bernard, who have been making wire toys since they were young boys. They now export their toys all over the world.

When the boy on the bicycle is pushed along the ground, his arms beat out a rhythm on the shoe polish lid. He is dressed in clothes sewn from scraps of cloth and his hat is a lid from an oil bottle.

The shaped wheel axle is a clever way to make parts of the model move up and down. The mechanism is a little tricky to master. However, when you have successfully made the bicycle drummer, you may like to go on to design your own wire toy with moving parts.

Make a bicycle drummer

You will need: two wire coathangers · pliers · tin lid · lengths of flexible wire · pencil · thick brown or black tights · needle and thread · material · bottle top · florist's wire

1 Untwist a coathanger with pliers and straighten. Bend one end in a circle inside the tin lid. Bend the next 10 cm to form a support for the drum. Hold with pliers and bend to form a complete circle 7 cm in diameter.

Bend the wire upwards to make a seat for the drummer, and finally backwards to form the handle.

2 Snip the hook from the second coathanger and straighten. Form the wheels and shaped axle from this wire. Make sure the wheels are bigger than the axle shapes so that the axles do not hit the ground.

3 With 4 metres of flexible wire form the body and neck. Leave twisted ends at back. Form arms using 2.8-m pieces. Twist ends around a pencil several times to make drumsticks. Make loops at elbows and ends, and bend at shoulders.

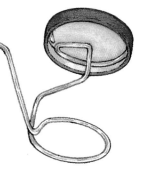

4 Make two arm-movers from 1.3-m pieces. Loop at both ends. Form legs from 3.6-m piece of wire.

5 To make head, stuff pieces of tights into toe of one leg. Push wire neck into head. Sew neck tightly. Twist rest of tights leg around body. Push arms through shoulder loops and close end loops. Push legs through hip loops.

6 Dress your drummer from scraps of material. Add a bottle top for a hat.

7 To assemble, twist end of body wire around 'seat' and ends of legs around bottom circle. Wind florist's wire around bottom circle and under axle at both sides to hold in place. Leave axle free to turn. Loop arm movers through elbows and around shapes, fixing in place with more florist's wire.

Toys to catch the wind

All over the world toys have been invented to catch the power of the wind. Paper kites on a bamboo frame may have originated in China about 3,000 years ago, although there are also records of a Greek kite inventor, Archytas of Tarentum, in 400 BC. The Chinese kites were not toys, however. They were used to measure the distance between armies in a battle or to carry a rope across a dangerous river. Soldiers also used 'whistling' kites to scare the enemy. They were fitted with tightened strings that wailed eerily in the wind.

Today kite flying is a popular sport in Japan. Annual festivals are held involving battles between enormous kites that are flown by whole teams of flyers. Powdered glass is dusted onto the kite's string. The aim is to cut through the string of an opponent's kite and capture the kite where it falls.

Make a mini-kite

1 Lay a stick on folded newspaper. With a craft knife, whittle off the top layer, leaving a flat surface. Turn the stick over and do the same to the other side. Repeat with the other sticks. Shorten one stick to 19 cm.

You will need: five green 30-cm bamboo garden sticks • newspaper • craft knife • layout or copy paper • poster paints • large brush • PVA glue mixed with water • strong glue • cotton thread • silk thread • needle • string • very long length of nylon thread (or a prepared reel from a kite shop)

2 Cut a piece of layout paper, 19.5 x 24.5 cm. Fold in edges by 1 cm all round and then open again. Paint a design on the front with poster paints and leave to dry.

3 With a large brush, paint all over the back of the paper with glue mixture. Add a dot of strong glue at each corner.

4 Lay the five sticks across the sticky surface as shown. Fold paper edges back over the stick ends and press firmly. Tie the sticks at the centre and at top corners with cotton thread.

5 Paint glue mixture over the decorated front. As it dries, the paper will become taut like a drum.

6 Thread a needle with silk thread. On the front of the kite, pierce paper at top right-hand corner and tie end of silk firmly around bamboo sticks. Repeat on left, forming a loop 44 cm long. Attach a third silk strand to the middle stick, 7 cm from bottom. Tie the other end to the top of the loop, forming a triangle.

7 Cut three 100-cm lengths of string and tie at one end. Attach this tail with silk to the centre back of the kite. To fly your kite, attach nylon thread to the triangle of silk thread.

Get together with a group of friends, your class at school or a youth group, and try to make a really big kite to fly as a team. You will need to find a book on kite-making, and a big windy space in which to try out your creation.

Useful information

United Kingdom

Some helpful addresses

Bangladesh Centre of
East London
185a Cannon Street Road
LONDON E1 2LX

Barnet Multicultural Study Centre
Barnet Teachers' Centre
451 High Road
Finchley
LONDON N12 0AS

Bethnal Green Museum of
Childhood
Cambridge Heath Road
LONDON E2

Japan Information and
Cultural Centre
101–104 Piccadilly
LONDON W1V 9FN

The Russian Experience, GNBA
Bawtry Hall, Bawtry
DONCASTER DN10 6JH
(Russian nesting dolls)

Equipment and materials

Hobby Stores
39 Parkway
LONDON NW1
(balsa wood and craft equipment)

Museums

The Museum of Mankind
6 Burlington Gardens
Piccadilly
LONDON W1

National Toy Museum
Rottingdean Grange
Rottingdean
BRIGHTON

Pitt Rivers Museum
University of Oxford
Parks Road
OXFORD

Pollock's Toy Museum
1 Scala Street
LONDON W1

Toys for sale

Jackson Contra-Banned
Unit 2, Gatehouse Enterprise
Centre, Albert Street, Lockwood
HUDDERSFIELD HD1 3QD
*(mail order catalogue and
education packs)*

Joliba
47 Colston Street
BRISTOL BS1 5AX
*(arts from Mali & Niger Bend – mail
order and education supplement)*

Kirsten Baybars Toy Shop
7 Mansfield Road
LONDON NW3

Kite Corner
657 Watford Way
Mill Hill
LONDON NW7 3JR

Oxfam Education
46a Church Street
Stoke Newington
LONDON N16 0LU
('drop-in time' Wednesdays 2–7pm)

The Shaker Shop
27 Harcourt Street
LONDON W1H 1DT
(traditional North American dolls)

Soma Books Ltd
38 Kennington Lane
LONDON SE11 4LS
(Indian craft and book list)

World Art
164 Brook Road
LONDON E5 8AP
*(crafts from Zimbabwe and
Southern Africa)*

Books

*The Art and Craft of
Papier Mâché*
Juliet Bawden (Mitchell Beazley)

Art of the World series (Methuen)

Arts & Crafts of South America
Lucy Davies and Mo Fini (Tumi)

Handcrafts of India
Kamaladevi Chattopadhyay
(Indian Council for Cultural
Relations)

How to Start Carving
Charles Graveney (Studio Vista)

The Joy of Making Indian Toys
Sudarshan Khanna
(National Book Trust India))

Toys and Games
Ruth Thomson (Watts Books)

The World of Toys
Dr Josef Kandert (Hamlyn)

Australia

Alderson Craftmart
264 Railway Parade
Kogarah NSW 2217

Aldex Industries Pty Ltd
64 Violet Street
Revesby NSW 2212

Burwood Craft Supplies
173 Burwood Road
Burwood NSW 2134

The Cradt Company
272 Victoria AAvenue
Chatswood NSW 2067

Hobby Co.
197 Pitt Street
Sydney NSW 2000

Powerhouse Museum
Harris Street
Ultimo NSW 2007

Glossary

apprentice Someone who learns a skill from an expert.

balsa Very soft, light wood from the balsa tree.

burial site A place where many people have been buried.

charioteer A person who drove a horse-drawn racing cart called a chariot.

charm An object which is believed to have magic powers.

crochet A method of making fabric by looping wool or cotton with a hook.

flamboyant Brightly coloured and decorated.

fragment A small piece which has broken off something.

livestock Live animals that are kept for their milk, wool or meat.

***Matyroshka* doll** A traditional painted wooden doll from the countries of the former Soviet Union. Each doll is hollow and fits inside another one.

Mesolithic A period of ancient history that was part of the Stone Age.

Mesopotamia An ancient kingdom on the site of modern Iraq.

Middle Ages A period of history between AD 1000 and 1400.

mural A picture that is painted directly onto a wall.

Pioneer One of the people who travelled westwards across North America to start up new settlements and towns.

pre-Columbian A period in South American history before the continent was discovered by the explorer Christopher Columbus.

raffia Fibre from the palm tree. It is used to tie plants and make hats and baskets.

replica A copy.

sage A wise person.

tap tap A truck that is used to transport people and their luggage in Haiti.

whittle To carve with a knife.

worry doll A tiny doll from Guatemala in Central America. Children believe that worry dolls will take away their worries.

Index

Additional photographs:

page 10 (top): James Merrell, from *Living with Folk Art* by Nicholas Barnard, published by Thames and Hudson, London, 1991.